Can I tell you about OCD?

Can I tell you about...?

The "Can I tell you about...?" series offers simple introductions to a range of limiting conditions. Friendly characters invite readers to learn about their experiences of living with a particular condition and how they would like to be helped and supported. These books serve as excellent starting points for family and classroom discussions.

Other subjects covered in the "Can I tell you about...?" series

ADHD

Asperger Syndrome

Asthma

Dementia

Dyslexia

Epilepsy

Parkinson's Disease

Selective Mutism

Stuttering/Stammering

Can I tell you about OCD?

A guide for friends, family and professionals

AMITA JASSI
Foreword by Isobel Heyman
Illustrated by Sarah Hull

Jessica Kingsley *Publishers*
London and Philadelphia

First published in 2013
by Jessica Kingsley Publishers
116 Pentonville Road
London N1 9JB, UK
and
400 Market Street, Suite 400
Philadelphia, PA 19106, USA

www.jkp.com

Copyright © Amita Jassi 2013
Foreword copyright © Isobel Heyman 2013
Illustrations copyright © Sarah Hull 2013

Library of Congress Cataloging in Publication Data
Jassi, Amita.
Can I tell you about OCD? : a guide for friends, family,
and professionals / Amita Jassi ; foreword by
Isobel Heyman ; illustrated by Sarah Hull.
pages cm.
Audience: 7+
Includes bibliographical references and index.
ISBN 978-1-84905-381-5 (alk. paper)
1. Obsessive-compulsive disorder in children--Juvenile
literature. I. Hull, Sarah (Illustrator), illustrator.
II. Title. III. Title: Can I tell you about obsessive-compulsive disorder?
RJ506.O25J37 2013
616.85'22700835--dc23
2012051512

British Library Cataloguing in Publication Data
A CIP catalogue record for this book is available from the British Library

ISBN 978 1 84905 381 5
eISBN 978 0 85700 736 0

Printed and bound in Great Britain

Contents

Foreword

This little book fills an important gap in the current literature available for children and teenagers with obsessive compulsive disorder. It really tackles in a clear and accessible way one of the most distressing and less well-understood aspects of OCD: unpleasant obsessions.

Awareness of OCD in young people has increased in the last decade, and there has been encouraging expansion of psychological treatments, specifically cognitive behaviour therapy (CBT) incorporating exposure with response prevention. But the type of OCD which is most represented in books for children, or in films and on television, features the common symptoms such as fears of germs and dirt, with compulsions of repeated washing.

This book breaks new ground by dealing with one of the less well-known features of OCD: intrusive distressing obsessions.

Many young people are haunted by distressing obsessions, in particular unwanted thoughts on unpleasant or taboo themes. These can include fears of harm coming to themselves or others, worries that they may hurt others, unwanted or unpleasant sexual thoughts, and thoughts that offend their religious beliefs.

This book will help young people who know someone with OCD to better understand what their friend or family member may be going through, and it can be used by parents, teachers and other professionals to increase their own understanding, as well as the understanding of the children in their care. It will also help children with these types of symptoms realise that this is just another common manifestation of OCD...and that it can be treated in just the same way. And, even more importantly,...they are not alone. Many children with these distressing thoughts think they are uniquely strange or bad, and do not realise that this is a well-recognised OCD symptom.

There is a common belief that OCD which is dominated by unpleasant obsessions rather than the more usual compulsions, such as washing or checking, is very difficult to treat with CBT. Dr Jassi helps dispel this myth but showing that the same techniques of teaching a child to identify unpleasant thoughts and face them, while resisting rituals or avoidance, really does work.

Dr Jassi has ten years of clinical and research experience in working with people with OCD, and her practical and common sense approach leads children gently to recovery. This book will not only be a great relief to young people and their friends and families, who are trying to understand and deal with obsession, but also to therapists.

Dr Isobel Heyman MBBS PhD FRCPsych
Honorary Consultant Psychiatrist to the
National OCD Service for Young People, Maudsley
Hospital London, and Consultant Psychiatrist,
Great Ormond Street Hospital for Children

Acknowledgements

I would like to thank the many friends, family and colleagues who have helped me over the years to get me to the place of being able to write this book; there are too many people to mention, but you know who you are.

Thank you to all my colleagues and friends at the National Specialist Young Person's OCD Clinic at the Maudsley Hospital. In particular, Faye Barrow, Jacinda Cadman, Isobel Heyman and Georgina Krebs, who read manuscripts of the book and gave invaluable feedback and ideas. Thanks, Isobel, for asking me to write the book in the first place!

I wish to thank all the young people and families who I have had contact with over the years in the clinic. You have all have inspired me in many different ways and have shown strength and courage in fighting OCD. Thank you to Jonathan Davies and Claudia Semadeni who read the book and gave helpful feedback.

Finally, I would like to acknowledge the ongoing support, encouragement and love given by my parents and my brothers, Ammit and Anil. Thank you for always being there.

"Hi my name is Katie and I am 13 years old. OCD wanted me to keep it a secret, but I would like to tell you about my OCD."

"OCD is an anxiety disorder that's really common in people around my age; about 1 or 2 in every 100 people have OCD. That means in my school, there are probably 10–20 people with it, not just me! I don't know who they are; I guess it's not always obvious who has OCD. Anyone can get it; boys, girls and people from anywhere in the world can have it.

OCD stands for obsessive compulsive disorder. I get thoughts and pictures popping into my head over and over again, which make me feel scared, worried and sometimes embarrassed. I also sometimes get urges to do things even though I don't really want to do them. These are called obsessions. OCD makes me feel like I have to do something to stop the obsessions coming true or to get rid of the anxiety. The things I have to do for OCD are called compulsions. Obsessions and compulsions can get in the way of the things I want to do. OCD affects people in different ways, they might get different thoughts to me, or have different things which OCD makes them do, but it's still called OCD."

"Obsessions are intrusive, they make me feel scared. They keep popping up and they make me feel like I need to do something to stop them coming true, or to get them to go away."

"People have different types of obsessions;
I have put a list of common OCD
obsessions at the back of the book.

Everyone experiences things that pop into
their head now and then that they don't like
or don't want to come into their head. For me,
they come up more often than for someone
without OCD. The thoughts are annoying and
make me frightened. It is hard to get them to
stop or ignore them. I worry about something
awful happening to my parents and I would be
responsible if it did; I get pictures in my head
where I see something bad has happened to
them. I have other obsessions too and, like
lots of other people with OCD, my obsessions
have changed as I have got older, I also worry
whether I have harmed someone, I keep thinking
when I walk past people in the street or at a
train station that I might have pushed them.
When I do walk past, I feel an urge, which
makes me feel like I am about to do it; it is really
upsetting, as I know I would never do that and
I feel guilty for having these thoughts. I know
they don't make sense and that's why it can be
embarrassing to tell other people about them."

"Doing the compulsions makes me stressed,
but I worry my obsessions will come true
or won't go away if I do not do them."

"Compulsions or rituals are things I feel I have to do and I would feel really anxious if I did not do them. I have put a list of common OCD compulsions at the back of the book. These rituals are often triggered by the obsessions I have, and OCD makes me believe that if I do the rituals it will mean my fears will not come true and the obsessions will go away.

My OCD makes me do lots of different rituals. When I worry or get pictures of something unlucky or bad happening to my parents, I have to tap my hands four times against a surface (because four is my lucky number) or I have to repeat whatever I am doing at the time. OCD makes me believe that if I do this, then nothing bad will happen to my parents. If I get interrupted whilst doing rituals, I have to keep repeating them until it feels just right.

When I worry about something bad happening to my parents, I have to repeat the word 'lucky' in my head four times. Because these rituals are in my head they're called *mental rituals* and, unlike my tapping and repeating rituals, people can't see me doing them."

"OCD can make other people
do rituals for me, like answering
questions over and over."

"When OCD makes me worry if I have harmed someone when I am out, I feel I have to keep asking the person I am with whether I have hurt or pushed someone. Even if they tell me I didn't, I keep asking over and over to make sure, until the doubt and anxiety go away. This is a compulsion called *reassurance seeking*. Sometimes my friends and parents get really annoyed with me asking the same question over and over. I wish I didn't have to ask, but I am so scared that I might have hurt someone that I need to check with others.

I try to resist doing compulsions as people might think I'm strange when they see me do them. When I try not to do them, I feel like a volcano, and all the pressure keeps building and building and it feels like I am going to explode if I do not do them as soon as I get an obsession. It just feels easier to do the rituals when OCD wants me to."

"OCD makes me think that I'd be better just sitting in my bedroom on my own so I could avoid all the things that trigger my obsessions and compulsions."

"OCD makes me avoid going to certain places and doing certain things because I do not want to trigger obsessions, or have to keep repeating the same thing over and over again. I hate having the obsessions, so I try and find ways not to have them. If I have to start doing rituals where other people could see me, I feel embarrassed and ashamed about people seeing me do them, so sometimes it feels easier to not go out or be around people. Sometimes I try to make excuses not to go to school as I end up doing tapping rituals at school and I do not want other people to see me, so I would rather stay at home.

When I do go out with my friends, I try to stay away from people due to my worries about pushing people or hurting them in some way. It is hard though as I have to try and get on with my life, and I want to do the things everyone else my age does. It can really get me down sometimes.

I am not trying to be difficult or trying to get out of doing things but OCD makes me feel I have no choice but to avoid things."

"Going to the doctor to tell him about OCD was difficult, but it helped me get the support I needed."

"I kept OCD a secret for a long time as I did not know how to explain what was going on because it was so confusing. My teachers and parents started to notice my rituals and that I was anxious most of the time so my parents took me to see my doctor.

My doctor asked me about how I was feeling and what I was doing. He told us that it sounded like OCD and he asked the child mental health services to see me to do an assessment. My parents and I met with a psychologist and psychiatrist and they asked me lots of different questions about what compulsions I was doing and the obsessions I was having. They also asked me how it made me feel and what it was stopping me from doing or enjoying. It was hard to talk about it, but they made me feel safe and they told me they had seen lots of people with OCD.

At the assessment I was told lots of people have thoughts they don't like and people have habits and do rituals, but as my obsessions and compulsions took longer than an hour a day and they were causing me distress and getting in the way of the things I wanted to do, this meant I had OCD."

"There is no known cause of OCD;
it is nobody's fault I got it. The
good news is that it is treatable
and you can get better from it."

"Even though people don't know why I got OCD, there are some things that might have made me more likely to have it. Anxiety and mood problems can run in families and people with OCD worry too much if they get a bad or unpleasant thought. Everyone gets unwanted thoughts, but I am more sensitive to them and get more upset when I have them.

Scientists also think people with OCD may have differences in a brain chemical called serotonin. These chemicals talk to each other and pass messages, but although no one knows exactly how it works, it seems that sometimes the serotonin in my brain may be underactive. I get 'brain hiccups' where the messages and thoughts between the chemicals get stuck; these are the obsessions.

Stressful events can trigger OCD. Mine started when I first went to secondary school and I found the change of schools difficult. There were some boys who bullied me at school too. It was around that time I noticed I kept getting horrible thoughts coming into my head and that I felt I needed to do rituals to make them go away. After that, I kept getting new obsessions and compulsions and my OCD got stronger and stronger."

"I really try to control my OCD at school, but it very difficult."

"I used to love school but now OCD makes some things hard for me. When obsessions pop into my head, it is really hard to concentrate in class, so I often miss what the teachers are saying. All I can think about is trying to do my ritual. It's really distracting when I have to do mental rituals in class. Teachers sometimes tell me off because they may ask me a question that I have not heard because OCD has been in my head. I get really tired as I have obsessions and have to do compulsions, so that can make it hard to focus too.

The repeating rituals can affect my schoolwork as I end up re-writing and re-reading until OCD says it is ok to move on. It means I take longer to do my school and homework and sometimes I don't finish things on time.

I get really uncomfortable when OCD triggers the tapping or repeating movement rituals. Other kids in my class really notice them, especially if I am tapping loudly and they sometimes pick on me. It is really hard to explain to people why I do these things, as I do not want them to know I have OCD."

"OCD affects my life in so many different ways and it can be hard for me to explain to people or for others to understand why I do what I do."

"At home, I argue with my parents and brother quite a lot when they are trying to get me to go out or do things around the house. They think I'm just being lazy when I say I can't do things. I don't want to do much around the house because I get stuck repeating things if an obsession has popped into my head. Sometimes when my parents don't do what OCD wants or I don't do my ritual right, I shout or throw things around the house. It's not what I would usually do and I always feel bad afterwards, but it's because I feel anxious.

My parents sometimes get annoyed with me if I ask questions over and over when OCD is tricking me into thinking I have hurt someone. They give me the answers, but sometimes OCD just keeps making me ask over and over until it is satisfied.

I think it was really hard for my family to work out that I had an anxiety problem at first; they thought I was doing these things on purpose. I was scared to tell, but once I explained a bit more about it, and they could see how much it upset me, they took me to see a doctor."

"OCD makes it hard to enjoy
my time with my friends and they
sometimes get impatient with me."

"I have only told my best friends that I have OCD. It was really hard to tell them but I am glad I did. I do not get to go out as much as I'd like with my friends as I am always scared about obsessions being triggered or doing rituals in public and other people seeing me. My mates ask me to come for sleep-overs or come to parties, my parents say I can go but OCD says no! It's really good that my friends understand that and they're always encouraging me to come out if I can.

Before I had OCD, I used to spend lots of time with all my friends but now my OCD makes it so hard. Sometimes they will be talking and laughing, but my OCD might be making me do mental rituals and then I lose track of the conversation, so my friends think I don't care about what they are talking about, even though I do. Sometimes I annoy them when OCD tells me to seek reassurance from them a lot. It's so frustrating and I sometimes do not feel as close to my friends as I used to be."

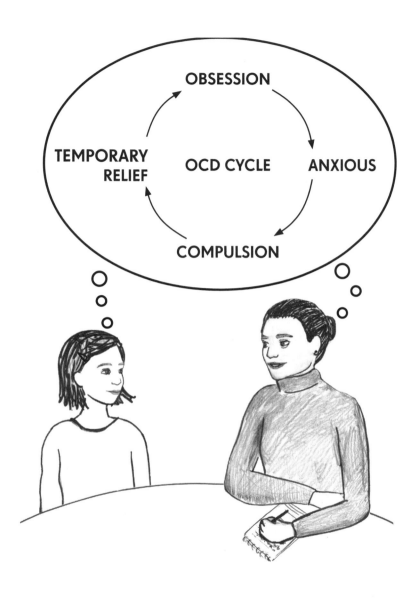

"CBT can be hard, but I am learning how to fight OCD by resisting compulsions step by step and learning my obsessions do not come true."

"CBT stands for cognitive behaviour therapy. It is a talking and doing treatment for OCD; I meet with my therapist once a week for an hour. My parents come to my sessions. Sometimes they stay for the whole time or other times they come in at the end so my therapist can tell them what I have done and how they can help.

At the beginning of CBT, we focused on learning more about how OCD and anxiety work. I learnt about the vicious cycle of OCD; that, by doing rituals, I was never learning if my worries would come true or not. I learnt that if I resisted rituals, then my anxiety would reduce over time by itself. If I kept practising this, then my therapist said it would get easier each time.

We developed a *hierarchy* where I listed everything OCD made me do and then I had to rate how anxious I would feel if I did not do the ritual using my *anxiety rating scale.* This is used as a guide as to what rituals to try and tackle step by step, starting with the easier ones and moving to harder ones once my confidence builds up. This made fighting back seem much easier."

"The main tool in fighting OCD is called *exposure with response prevention (ERP).* This means facing a feared situation that triggers an obsession (exposure) and then resisting doing the ritual (response prevention)."

"In sessions, I use my hierarchy to pick a situation to face which makes me anxious because of the obsession, and then I try to resist doing the ritual. By doing these tasks, I am learning that my anxiety goes up first and then it comes down all by itself without me having to do a ritual. I have also learnt that the more I practise each task, the easier it gets each time.

Doing these tasks helps me to understand that obsessions do not come true if I do not do what OCD says. I did not believe my therapist at first, but now I have tried it out a few times, I realise OCD was just playing tricks on me. I have to practise tasks in between sessions for homework. This is so I get loads of practice and my parents help me with this too.

In the last sessions we will make a plan to make sure OCD stays away when I am better. This is called a relapse prevention plan."

"I will not be on medication forever; it will just help me to use the tools I learn in CBT."

"CBT can help me get rid of OCD, but sometimes people need medication too. My doctor told me medication is like arm bands when you are learning to swim or stabilisers when you are learning to ride a bike. You need them when you are learning but eventually they can come off.

Medication can help when you are learning to fight OCD using CBT tools; it can make it a bit easier to deal with the anxiety when doing ERP (exposure with response prevention) tasks. If CBT works like it is meant to and I stay well for about 6–12 months after finishing treatment, then the doctors have said I can gradually start to reduce medication and then stop taking it."

"Some people just take medication and do not do CBT, but if you can it is better to learn CBT techniques as well. Then you have your own 'tool-kit' to help fight OCD if it tries to come back. The best medicines for helping with OCD are called selective serotonin reuptake inhibitors (SSRIs). My doctor told me they increase the level of the brain chemical serotonin in the brain. This is why scientists think there might be lower levels of serotonin in the brains of people with OCD. Different people need different amounts of this medication and the doctors decide how much will help. Some people don't need medication at all when doing CBT, but having both is often the best way to fight OCD."

How family and friends can help

"OCD not only makes things hard for me, but also my friends and family. I have to get reassurance from them and OCD makes me avoid things they would like me to be involved in. It is hard because, if they let me avoid things, or give me reassurance, then it makes OCD stronger. However, if they don't do these things, or if they tell me off, it can make me really upset and can be very hard for me.

It is really important that my parents are involved in my CBT sessions. My therapist has explained to them how my OCD works, and now they help me with my tasks. They sometimes have to support me with doing ERP tasks at home or they may have to stop doing rituals for my OCD, for example by not giving reassurance. We have used my hierarchy to decide tasks together and my therapist talks to my parents about how to help me each week.

Some things my family and friends can do to help me are:

- Understand it is OCD and not me that is making me do rituals and making me upset and anxious.

- Understand how OCD works.

- Be calm and considerate.

- My parents give me the same rules as my brother, so I know the boundaries at home.

- My parents praise and reward me when I have managed to resist OCD.

- My parents help me with my CBT and come to my sessions.

- Not stopping doing things for OCD all at once, but planning tasks with me in steps that I can manage."

How I can be helped at school

"OCD doesn't always get in the way for people at school. For me, school was hard because I wanted to avoid going as much as possible, and I was finding it hard to concentrate in lessons. Because I found it tough at school, my therapist has contacted my school to help them understand OCD and how they can help. She gave them some ideas to help me:

- There should be regular contact between my parents, school and my therapist so they can all help me manage my OCD step by step according to what tasks I am doing in my CBT sessions.

- Teachers need to know what symptoms come up in school and how to deal with them, i.e. be patient.

- Sometimes they let me have some time out of the classroom if I am struggling so my anxiety level can come down and I can get on with my work.

- At the moment they have given me extra time to do my homework because of re-reading and re-writing rituals and I will have extra time in exams. I won't need this forever, but it helps until I can get better from my OCD.

- My teachers keep an eye on me and make sure that no one is picking on me at school. The teachers can recognise my rituals and look out for bullies.

- The school did a lesson on mental health and OCD which helped people understand it better, but I decided I did not want other people to know I had it."

Common obsessions and compulsions

OBSESSIONS

- *Contamination*
  e.g. concerns about dirt, illness, environmental contaminants, sticky substances.

- *Aggressive*
  e.g. fear that might harm self or others, violent images, act on unwanted impulses.

- *Sexual*
  e.g. inappropriate sexual thoughts, images, impulses.

- *Hoarding/Saving*
  e.g. fear of losing things.

- *Magical/Superstitious*
  e.g. lucky/unlucky numbers colours and words.

- *Somatic*
  e.g. excessive concern with illness, disease, particular aspect of appearance.

- *Religious*
  e.g. fear of offending religious objects, excessive concern with right/wrong.

- *Miscellaneous*
  e.g. needing to know/remember, fear of saying certain things.

COMPULSIONS

- *Washing/Cleaning*
  e.g. excessive or ritualised hand washing, toileting, grooming, cleaning items.

- *Checking*
  e.g. checking locks, that nothing terrible will/has happened, mistakes.

- *Repeating*
  e.g. re-reading, repeating routine activities, re-writing.

- *Counting*
  e.g. objects, certain numbers, words.

- *Ordering/Arranging*
  e.g. need for symmetry/evening up.

- *Hoarding/Saving*
  e.g. difficulty throwing things away, saving bits of paper, string, etc.

- *Excessive games/Superstitious behaviours*
  e.g. touching object a certain number of times, stepping over certain spots.

- *Rituals involving other persons*
  e.g. asking parent to repeatedly answer a question, asking them to check.

- *Miscellaneous*
  e.g. mental rituals, needing to touch, tap or rub, blinking, staring.

Other disorders related to OCD

TIC DISORDERS

Tic disorders are classified as follows: *transient tic disorder* (consists of multiple motor and/or phonic tics with duration of at least 4 weeks, but less than 12 months), *chronic tic disorder* (either single or multiple motor or phonic tics, but not both, which are present for more than a year), *Tourette syndrome* (when both motor and phonic tics are present for more than a year) and *tic disorder not otherwise specified* (tics are present, but do not meet the criteria for any specific tic disorder). Tics are sudden, repetitive, nonrhythmic movements (motor tics) and utterances (phonic tics). Motor tics are movement-based tics, while phonic tics are involuntary sounds produced by moving air through the nose, mouth or throat.

BODY DYSMORPHIC DISORDER (BDD)

People with BDD have excessive concern about and preoccupation with a perceived defect of their physical features. The person complains of a defect in either one feature or several features of their body, or vaguely complains about their general appearance, which causes psychological distress that causes clinically significant distress or impairs occupational or social functioning.

TRICHOTILLOMANIA

Trichotillomania is defined as a self-induced and recurrent loss of hair. People who have it report an increasing sense of tension before pulling the hair and gratification or relief when pulling the hair.

MAJOR DEPRESSIVE DISORDER

Major depressive disorder is characterised by depressed mood or a loss of interest or pleasure in daily activities consistently for at least a two week period. This mood is a change from the person's normal mood and it can affect people's social, occupational, educational or other important functioning.

OTHER ANXIETY DISORDERS

These can include *social anxiety disorder* (intense fear of social situations, causing considerable distress and impaired ability to function in at least some parts of daily life) and *generalised anxiety disorder* (characterised by excessive, uncontrollable and often irrational worry about everyday things that is disproportionate to the actual source of worry).

Recommended reading, organisations and websites

BOOKS

Derisley, J., Heyman, I., Robinson, S. and Turner, C. (2008) *Breaking Free from OCD: A CBT Guide for Young People and Their Families*. London: Jessica Kingsley Publishers.

Written by leading experts on OCD, this step by step guide is written for adolescents with OCD and their families, to be used in home treatment or as a self-help book. It uses the principles of cognitive behavioural therapy (CBT) and is suitable for young people aged 10–16 years and their families.

Wagner, A. P. (2004) *Up and Down the Worry Hill*. New York: Lighthouse Press.

This book has been written for children and uses images and metaphors to explain OCD. It is clear and understandable for everyone.

Wells, J. (2006) *Touch and Go Joe*. London: Jessica Kingsley Publishers.

An honest and amusing account of a 15-year-old's battle with OCD. Will be of interest to anyone who has suffered from or knows someone who has OCD.

Wever, C. (1994) *The Secret Problem*. New South Wales: Shrink-Rap Press.

An excellent book for explaining OCD and the treatment to children aged 12 and under.

ORGANISATIONS AND WEBSITES

National Services: A resource for mental health professionals
Obsessive Compulsive Disorder Service
Michael Rutter Centre
Maudsley Hospital
De Crespigny Park
London SE5 8AZ
www.national.slam.nhs.uk/services/camhs/camhs-ocd
Phone: +44 (0)20 3228 5222

National Institute of Clinical Excellence (NICE)
Write guidelines and recommendations for treatments.
These are based on lots of studies and evidence to
see what treatments work best. There is information on
treatments for OCD for young people on the website.
1st Floor, 10 Spring Gardens
London SW1A 2BU
http://guidance.nice.org.uk
Email: nice@nice.org.uk
Phone: +44 (0)845 003 7780

OCD action
Suite 506-7 Davina House
137-149 Goswell Road
London EC1V 7ET
www.ocdaction.org.uk
Email: support @ocdaction.org.uk
Phone: +44 (0)845 390 6232

OCD-UK
PO Box 8955
Nottingham
NG10 9AU
http://ocduk.org
Email: support@ocduk.org
Phone: +44 (0)845 120 3778